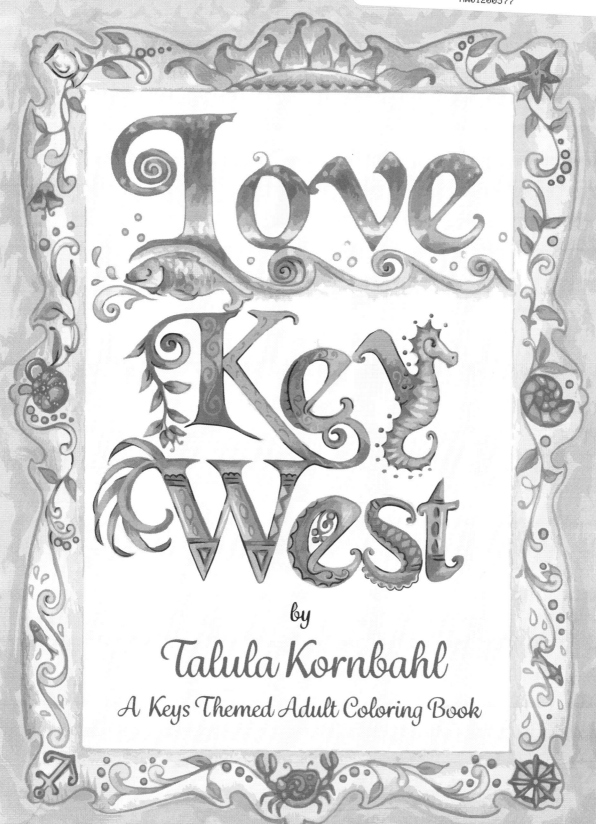

Love Key West

by

Talula Kornbahl

A Keys Themed Adult Coloring Book

idyl-wyld creative
Minneapolis, MN
ISBN-13:978-1543157758
ISBN-10:1543157750

Idyl-wyld.com
Talulakornbahl.com

This Book belongs to:

Lauren and Phillip Anderson

The Saltiest Mermaid in the Pond.
+ Merman

Please enjoy a little
"Couple time" on your
trip — or once you're home
again — with a cocktail and
a little coloring!
We love you!
XO, Heather, Matt, +
Harper
xoxo

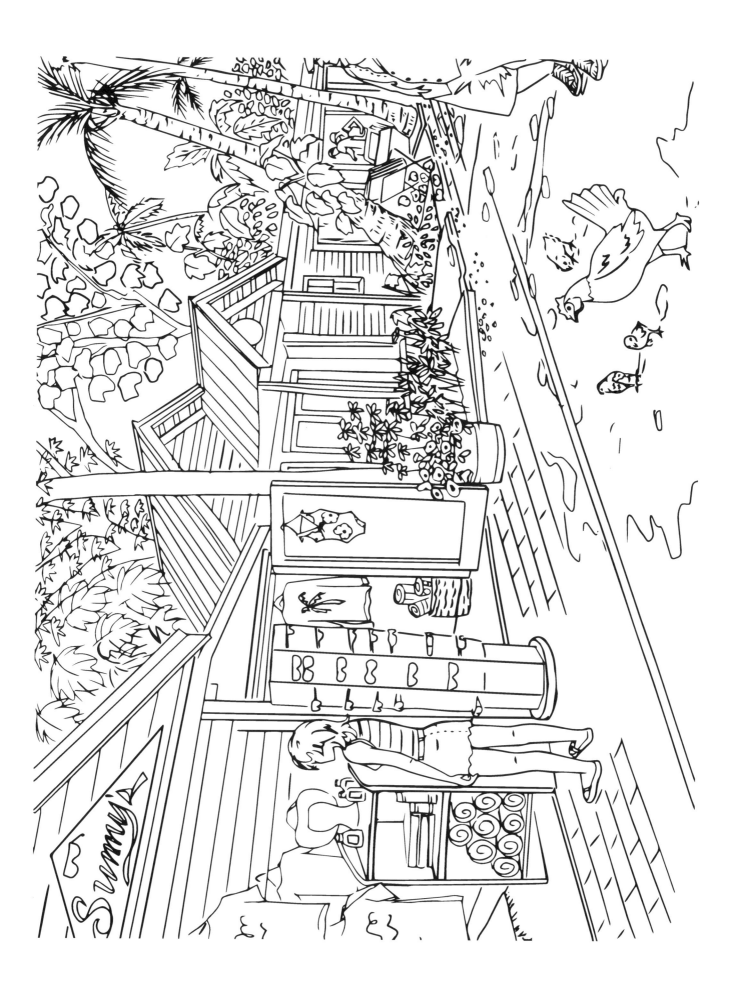

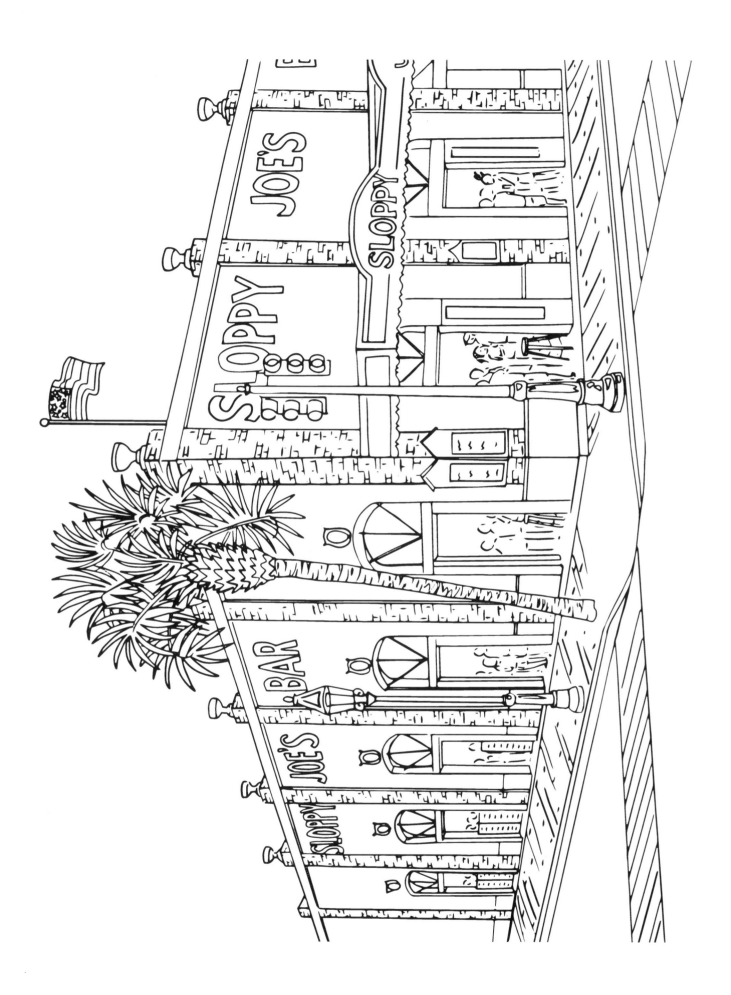

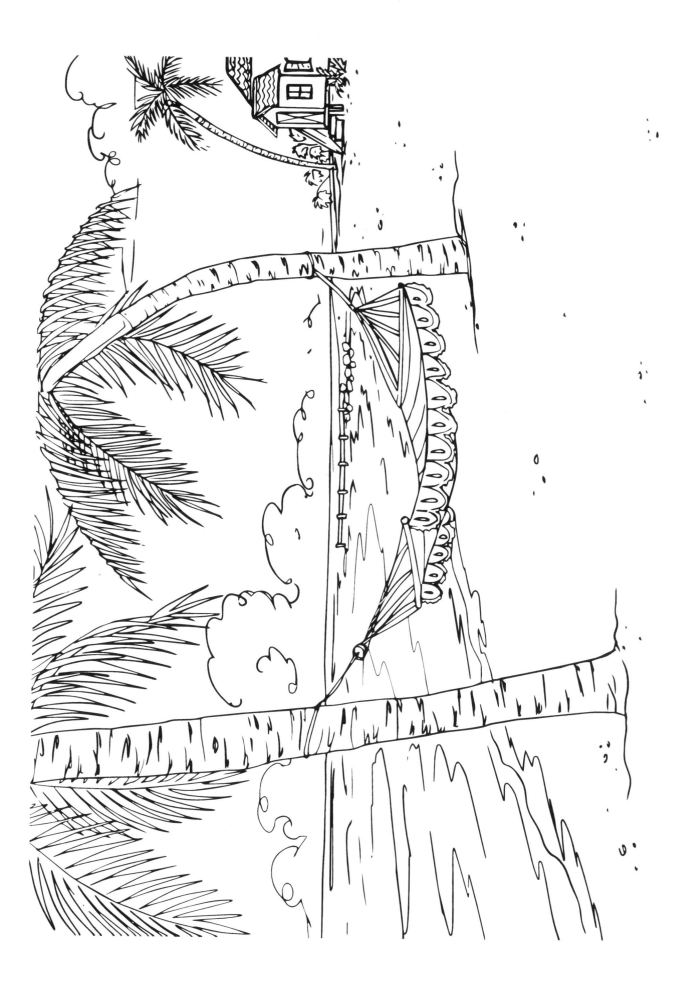

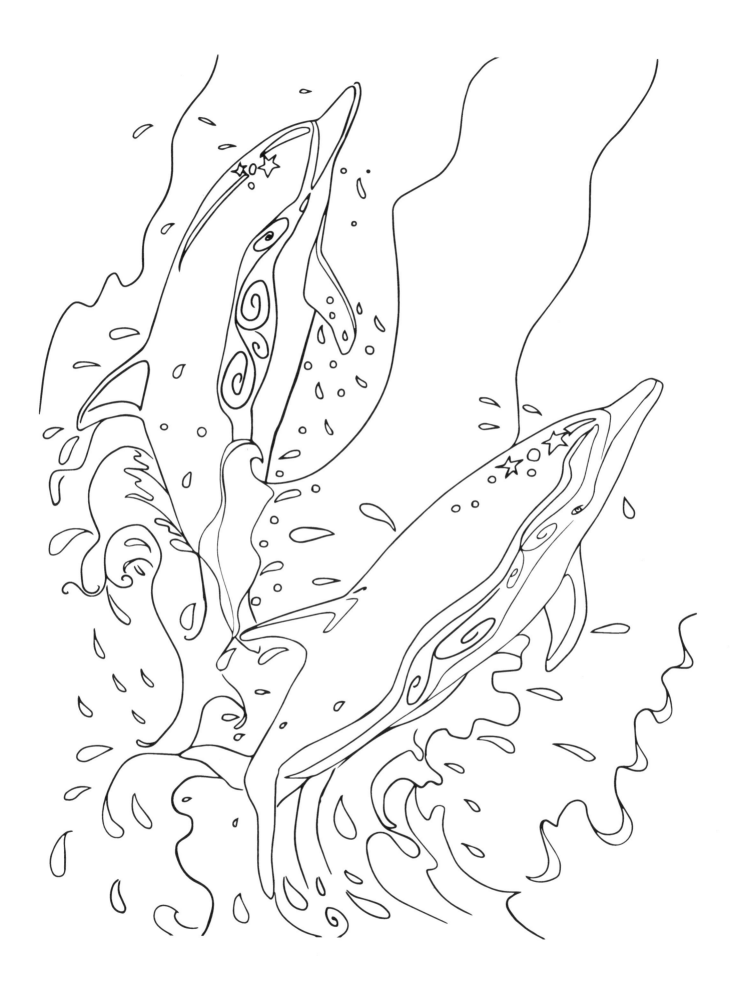

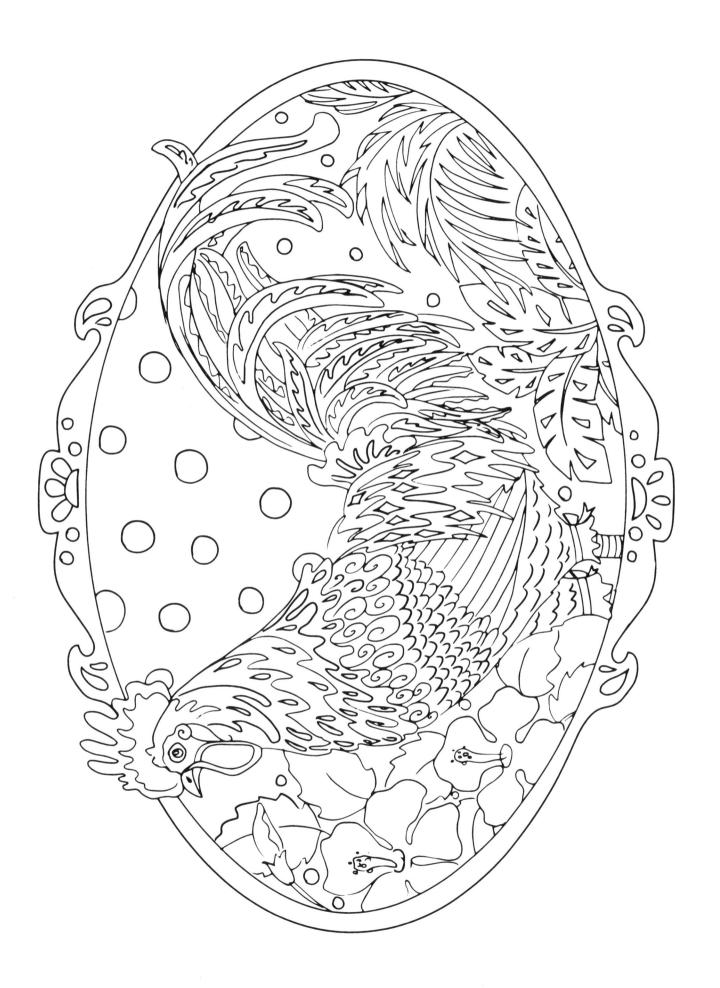

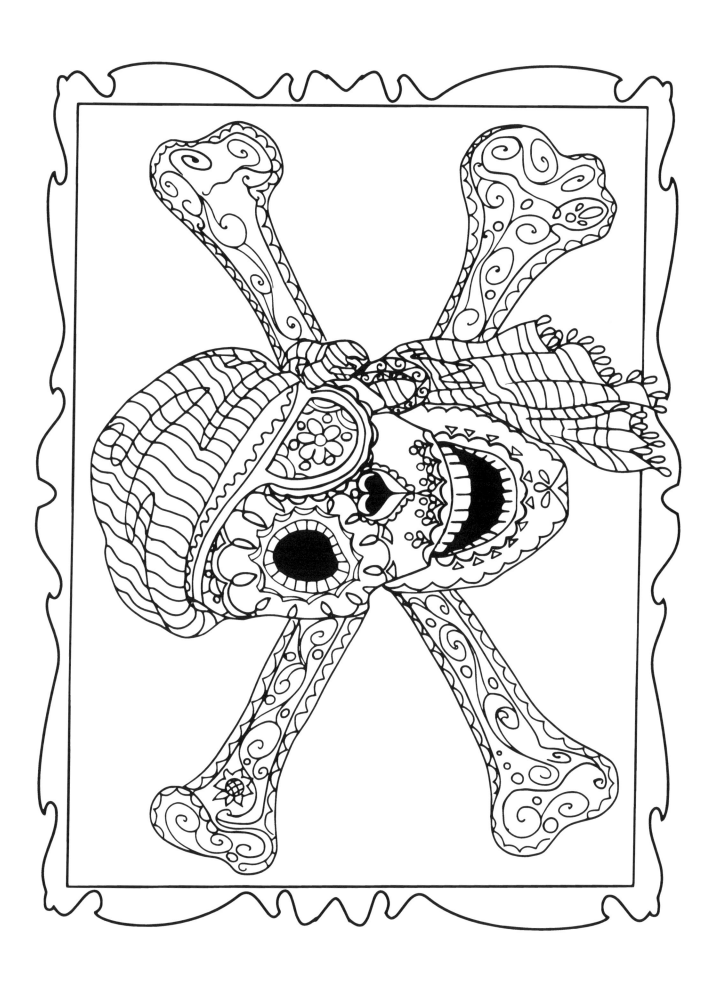

Thank you,
Mermaids and Salty Dogs!

Come Back Soon...